Venture Capital in Europe

Harry Cowie

FEDERAL TRUST REPORT

THE FEDERAL TRUST

The Federal Trust works through research and education towards the widening and deepening of the European Union as well as to enhance the European policy of the United Kingdom

The Trust conducts enquiries, promotes seminars and conferences and publishes reports and teaching materials on the European dimension.

Up-to-date information about the Federal Trust can be found on the internet at www.fedtrust.co.uk.

The Trust is the UK member of TEPSA (the Trans-European Policy Studies Association).

The Federal Trust is a registered charity and expresses no political view of its own.

Among the Trust's most recent publications are Andrew Duff, *The Unforeseeable Circumstances of Mr Gordon Brown* (1999); Charles Jenkins, *Paying for an Enlarged European Union* (1999); Andrew Duff (ed.), *Understanding the Euro*, Foreword by Kenneth Clarke, 1998; and Ian Davidson, *Jobs and the Rhineland Model*, 1998.

Published by the Federal Trust
Dean Bradley House
52 Horseferry Road
London SW1P 2AF

ISBN 0 901573 86 8

The Federal Trust is a Registered Charity
Marketing and Distribution by Kogan Page Ltd
Printed in the European Union

VENTURE CAPITAL IN EUROPE

Contents

Contents

Acknowledgment

Despite the launch of the euro in much of the European Union, there remain a number of important obstacles to the development of a truly integrated European capital market. These impediments are fiscal, economic, regulatory and cultural. The Federal Trust set up an inquiry in September 1998 to investigate how they might be overcome.

The study group met six times, and its membership included:

Sir Brian Corby	Chairman, Study Group	
Kate Bingham	Partner	Schroder Ventures Life Sciences Advisers (UK)
Jonathan Blake	Senior Partner	SJ Berwin & Co
Basil Butler	Chairman	KS Biomedix Holdings
Sir David Cooksey	Chairman	Advent Limited
Harry Cowie	Rapporteur, Study Group	Federal Trust
Chris Evans	Chairman	Merlin Ventures
Hermann Hauser	Director	Amadeus Capital Partners
Mr Ron Hollidge	Chief Executive	British Venture Capital Association
David McGlue	Executive Director	European Investment Fund
John Morley	Adviser to Director General	DG V, European Commission
Craig Pickering	Head of Asset Finance	The Finance and Leasing Association
Adrian Piper	Senior Adviser	Bank of England
Charles Richardson	Head of Corporate Affairs	3i
Keith Richardson	former Director General	European Round Table
Delphine Sallard	Administrator	DG II, European Commission
Paul Waller	Chairman	EVCA
Bill Wicksteed	Director	Segal Quince Wicksteed
David Wright	Cabinet of the President	European Commission
Stanislas Yassukovich	Chairman	EASDAQ

In addition, evidence was taken from Mr Graham Bannock, Bannock Consulting; Professor Colin Mason, University of Southampton; Mr David Votier, Carpmaels & Ransford.

Venture Capital in Europe is the latest in a series of Federal Trust studies on the theme of capital market integration. Earlier reports included *Jobs and the Rhineland Model* (1998), *Private Partnerships and Public Networks in Europe* (1996), *Network Europe and the Information Society* (1995), *The Pension Time Bomb in Europe* (1995), *Towards an Integrated European Capital Market* (1993), and *The Future of Corporate Tax in the European Community* (1991).

Harry Cowie, a Senior Research Fellow of the Trust, has been the Trust's prime mover in this area, and I am most grateful to him for his recent work as rapporteur. Sir Brian Corby, a Patron of the Trust, chaired the group with tact and wisdom. Richard Blackman, the Trust's Research Officer, acted as secretary of the study group and has helped steer it home.

Members of the study group served in their individual capacities and gave freely of their time. Individual members do not necessarily concur with all the views expressed in the report, but they support its general thrust and commend its publication. I am most grateful to them; and to DG V of the European Commission for a grant towards defraying the cost of this project.

The Trust welcomes comments about its reports. These should be addressed to me at the Federal Trust, Dean Bradley House, 52 Horseferry Road, London SW1P 2AF.

Andrew Duff
Director
March 1999

Glossary

Business Angels

Private individuals who invest directly in new and growing unquoted businesses. Business angels usually provide finance in return for an equity stake in the business, but may also provide other long-term finance. This capital can complement the venture capital industry by providing smaller amounts of finance (generally under €150,000) at an earlier stage than most venture capital firms are able to invest.

Early stage capital

Financing to companies before they initiate commercial manufacturing and sales, before they are generating a profit. Includes seed and start-up financing.

Equity

The ordinary share capital of a company.

Institutional investors

This term refers mainly to insurance companies, pension funds and investment companies collecting savings and supplying funds to the markets, but also to other types of institutional wealth (eg. endowment funds, foundations, etc.).

Initial Public Offering

Initial Public Offering (flotation, going public): the process of launching a public company for the first time by inviting the public to subscribe in its shares.

Management buy-out

Financing provided to enable current operating management and investors to acquire an existing product line or business.

Market capitalisation

The price of a stock multiplied by the total number of shares outstanding. The market's total valuation of a public company. By extension, the total valuation of companies listed on a stock market.

Microcredit

Very small loans, granted by specialised institutions.

Private equity

As opposed to public equity; investment in equity stake by private investors in companies not listed on a stock market.

Prospectus

A formal written offer to sell securities that sets forth the plan for a proposed business enterprise, or the facts concerning an existing one that an investor needs to make an informed decision.

Prudent-man regulation

Obligation of pension managers to invest as a prudent investor would do on his own behalf, in particular by carrying out sensible portfolio diversification, with no limits to portfolio distribution other than on self investment for pension funds financing defined benefit plans. The Netherlands, UK, Ireland, USA, Canada and Australia have such legislation.

Replacement capital

Purchase of existing shares in a company from another venture capital investment organisation or from another shareholder or shareholders.

Risk capital markets

Markets providing equity financing to a company during its early growth stages (start-up and development). In the framework of this communication, it covers three sorts of financing: informal investment by business angels; venture capital; stock markets specialised in SMEs and high growth companies.

Secondary market

Market where securities are bought and sold subsequent to original issuance. The existence of a flourishing, liquid, secondary market creates the conditions for a healthy primary market.

Security

A financial asset, including shares, government stocks, debentures, bonds, unit trusts and right to money lent or deposited.

Seed capital

Financing provided to research, assess and develop an initial concept.

Start-up capital

Provided to companies for product development and initial marketing.

Stock exchange (stock market)

A market in which securities are bought and sold. Its basic function is to enable public companies, governments and local authorities to raise capital by selling securities to investors.

Stock option

Option given to employees and/or managers to buy shares at a fixed price.

Venture capital

Investment in unquoted companies by venture capital firms who, acting as principals, manage individual, institutional or in-house money. Four main financing stages are identified in relation to the stages of development of a venture-backed company: early stage, expansion, replacement and buy-out. In the USA, the term 'venture capital' does not include most of the buy-out deals.

Venture capital funds

Closed-end funds, created to provide venture capital.

[Source: European Commission]

Abbreviations

AIM	Alternative Investment Market (London)
BAN	Business Angel Network
BVCA	British Venture Capital Association
CGT	Capital Gains Tax
EIB	European Investment Bank
EIF	European Investment Fund
EASDAQ	European Association of Securities Dealers Automated Quotation System
EMU	Economic and Monetary Union
EU	European Union
EVCA	European Private Equity & Venture Capital Association
ERISA	Employee Retirement Income Security Act
IPO	Initial Public Offering
IT	Information Technology
MBO	Mangement Buy Out
NASDAQ	National Association of Securities Dealers Automated Quotation System
SME	Small and Medium sized Enterprise
SEC	Securities Exchange Commission
UCITS	Undertaking for Collective Investment in Transferable Securities
VCT	Venture Capital Trusts

Foreword

Much attention has been paid over the last decade to the need to replicate within the European Union the dynamism which we have seen in the US economy. The extent of the references to our report bears this out.

A theme which is common to much of what we have considered is the difference between the European and American cultures — the institutionalised culture of much of the EU as compared with the individual, entrepreneurial culture of the US. Governments cannot command a change of culture, but they can act to create a climate which encourages such a change.

The recommendations we make are directed not only to the removal of barriers to entrepreneurship, but also to the introduction of measures which would provide clear incentives. To succeed requires action at regional, national and European levels.

Sir Brian Corby

Chairman of the Study Group

March 1999

1. Investment in European Innovation

Over the last twenty-five years the United States of America has pioneered a new technological revolution financed by a dynamic venture capital market. In the twenty years from 1975 two dozen American small enterprises have multiplied their annual turnover a hundred times to reach nearly $250 million, creating almost one and a half million jobs in the process. The pace of hi-tech growth continues to outstrip all other sectors. In 1991-95, 3% of firms accounted for 80% of job growth — 6 million out of an additional 7.7 million jobs in the American economy. The US now has a commanding world lead in biotechnology and information technology.[1]

In the European Union, meanwhile, private sector companies are less dynamic and governments have lacked confidence and cohesion about how to promote innovation. With some notable exceptions, European inventiveness has not delivered successful global companies.[2] Compared to the USA, small and medium sized enterprises in Europe find it difficult both to get started and to grow. European entrepreneurs tend to be faced with scepticism and ignorance in the banking sector, an absence of stock options, unreasonable legal and bureaucratic obstacles, a high cost of labour, unhelpful government agencies and unsympathetic tax authorities. How in these circumstances is it possible to grow global companies in Europe?

Clearly, Europe's general failure to exploit innovation has had adverse economic consequences, not least in the 'brain drain' of European inventors and a shift of corporate gravity across the Atlantic.

Concern about the obstinacy of structural unemployment in Europe has continued to rise since the notable 1993 White Paper of the European Commission of Jacques Delors, *Growth, Competitiveness, Employment*.[3] The Treaty of Amsterdam, agreed in June 1997, includes a new chapter on employment policy. A strategic meeting of the European Council in Luxembourg in November 1997 agreed a 'new approach' to combating unemployment. Evincing frustration at

Europe's seeming inability to foster sustainable growth, the leaders acknowledged the 'importance of the role that large pan-European risk capital markets can play in job creation', and sent the Commission away to produce proposals. The OECD, after a major study of the problem, called for wide reforms of the financial markets, as well as changes in R&D and the labour market.[4]

The Commission published an important and generally well-received communication to the Council in April 1998, *Risk Capital: A key to job creation in the European Union*. 'The political message', said the Commission, 'is a simple one':

> 'Developing risk capital in the European Union, leading towards the development of pan-European risk-capital markets is essential for major job creation in the EU. Although Economic and Monetary Union and the arrival of the Euro will create a more favourable environment and be a major catalyst for change, there remain a number of pernicious barriers — regulatory, economic, fiscal and cultural — that need to be addressed as a matter of urgency.
>
> 'In essence, what is at stake is the creation of a new entrepreneurial culture in Europe. The real political challenge is to provide the tools enabling technologies and financial instruments for a new generation of European entrepreneurs to start up and succeed. ...
>
> 'The Commission considers the provision of substantial pan-European risk-capital markets a necessary condition for this to happen'.[5]

The European Council discussed *Risk Capital* and an attached Action Plan (reproduced here in the Appendix) at Cardiff in June 1998 and again at Vienna in December. The Commission is to publish a progress report in mid-1999.

In *Risk Capital*, the European Commission identified six major obstacles. Top of the list is the fragmentation of the existing stock markets and secondary risk capital markets. The US has three principal stock markets and one coast to coast regulatory body, the Security and Exchange Commission (SEC). On the most restrictive definition, the European Union still has thirty-three regulated stock markets and eighteen regulatory organisations. As the Commission points out:

'This configuration reduces both the capitalisation and liquidity for each national market and hence 'exit' opportunities for the Venture Capitalist'.

In the Commission's opinion, the EU's institutional and regulatory framework provides neither the necessary incentives nor the required transparency, stability or predictability for the growth of pan-European risk capital. In particular, a harmonised, transparent tax structure is lacking at Community level which would help venture capital funds raise capital by marketing their units in other member states. The paucity of European technology-based firms is another key issue identified by the Commission, along with the lack of human resources and cultural differences.

Clearly, the absence of a large and truly integrated European capital market is not the only problem Europe faces.[6] But it is a key one, and this report examines what can be done to rectify the situation. We focus particularly on the provision of risk capital for young and small hi-tech firms. We do not cover all the issues raised by the Commission, but focus instead on the fragmentation of the European markets, the role of the financial institutions, tax incentives and the phenomenon of regional clusters.

In Table One we show the typical growth path of a hi-tech company.[7] In Table Two we show comparatively the volume of venture capital investment by stage.

We say least about the general culture of European enterprise because cultural change requires a lot of time and a rather profound shift in social and political attitudes. Nevertheless, there are some important (and somewhat over-looked) differences in entrepreneurial culture between Europe and the USA, especially California. There are a plethora of important cultural distinctions, too, within the European Union itself. We are not in favour of replacing such cultural diversity with a dull uniformity, but we do recognise that improved education, raised skills and enhanced aspirations form a vital part in the modernisation of all member and applicant states of the European Union.

TABLE ONE

Stages of Entrepreneurial Development

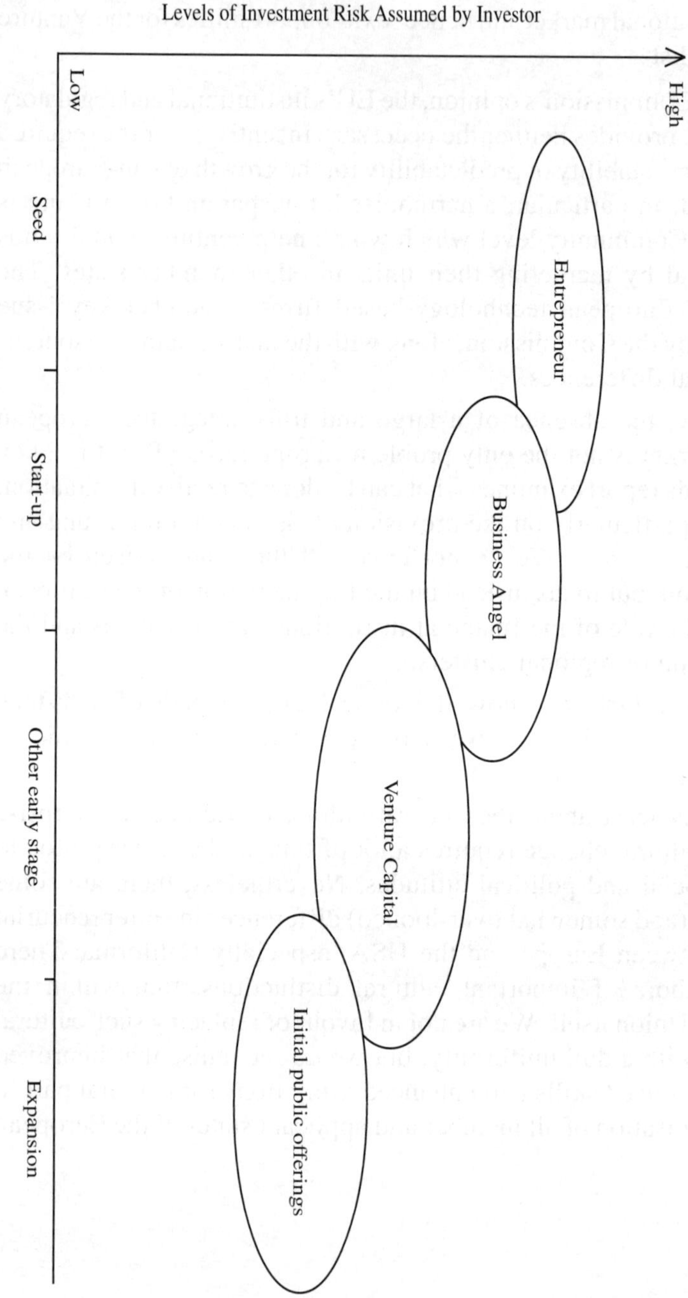

TABLE TWO

Volume of Venture Capital Investment by Investment Stage

Stage distribution of investments in 1997 (Ecu 1000)

	Seed and Start-up	Expansion and Replacement Capital	Buy-out	Total	GDP (Ecu million)	Early Stage	Later Stage
Austria	2,990	4,874	10,847	18,711	181,868	0.002%	0.003%
Belgium	29,793	144,491	4,680	178,964	213,884	0.014%	0.068%
Denmark	2,883	19,265	-	22,147	143,766	0.002%	0.013%
Finland	8,716	81,615	22,653	112,984	103,635	0.008%	0.079%
France	90,163	549,778	607,620	1,247,561	1,229,328	0.007%	0.045%
Germany	200,193	649,723	475,835	1,325,751	1,865,778	0.011%	0.035%
Greece	5,073	10,853	318	16,243	105,046	0.005%	0.010%
Ireland	1,368	33,427	1,417	36,212	64,121	0.002%	0.052%
Italy	73,764	333,831	195,532	603,126	1,010,946	0.007%	0.033%
Netherlands	151,908	310,597	297,034	759,538	320,077	0.047%	0.097%
Portugal	11,151	51,866	-	63,018	85,995	0.013%	0.060%
Spain	21,332	175,389	65,620	262,341	470,457	0.005%	0.037%
Sweden	4,497	81,553	264,881	350,931	202,418	0.002%	0.040%
UK	99,935	1,464,616	2,863,136	4,427,686	1,127,546	0.009%	0.130%
EU14	703,765	3,911,876	4,809,573	9,425,213	7,124,864	0.010%	0.055%
USA	3,030,000	7,343,687			6,682,102	0.045%	0.110%
Israel	98,784	153,468	44,100	296,351	88,200	0.112%	0.174%

Source: EVCA 1998 Yearbook, NVCA 1997 Annual Report, Israel Venture Association Yearbooks 1997 & 1998 (Bannock Consulting Estimates)

2. Institutional and Market Barriers

The American experience underlines the importance of the emergence of a pan-European risk capital market. Europe's national markets are too fragmented and small to provide the liquidity which is the hallmark of a successful stock market. Venture capitalists and other private investors may be reluctant to invest in new entrepreneurial companies unless they have the possibility of an exit route by way of a stock-market flotation. Highly successful ventures are sold off by way of an Initial Public Offering (IPO) which in the United States is largely performed through NASDAQ. At present only a minority of exits of European technology based firms are achieved through IPOs, as until recently stock markets in Europe have concentrated on large and medium sized companies and have not offered a specialist market for the flotation of the smaller firm. The situation has improved over the past two to three years, but Europe still has a very long way to go before it can replicate the US experience.

Institutional investors in several European countries are currently prevented from putting a significant part of their resources at the disposal of companies needing risk capital. By contrast, in the US pension funds and other financial institutions have provided close to half of venture capital in recent years, mainly by way of investment in venture capital companies. Because of the risks involved and the need to provide returns for their investors, venture capital companies require high rates of return and need to be able to dispose of at least half of their investment in a five to ten year framework.

Will the emergence of new regulated pan-European stock markets specialising in risk capital encourage continental European institutional investors to invest in specialist venture capital funds? In some cases, there are regulatory restrictions on the placement of funds by category of assets. In others, there are cultural factors which have made European investors more risk averse. Even in the UK where investment in equity is well established, the National Association of Pension

Funds estimates that only 0.75% of pension funds are invested in venture capital. A recent expert group reporting to the British Treasury commented:

> 'It is clear that changing the culture of institutional investment in venture capital would have a significant impact, providing it was married to the right mix of investment skills. It would spread the risk inherent in such investments. It would provide a larger pool of finance. It would increase the opportunities to identify those rare companies that have the potential for enormous growth, seen to such effect across the Atlantic'.[8]

NASDAQ

The NASDAQ market provides massive liquidity with a volume of over $20 billion a day in 1998, which is comparable to the New York Stock Exchange. It meets the special needs of high technology companies entering a growth phase, namely, long lead times before significant profitability, and investor reassurance that high risk can be matched with even higher potential gains. NASDAQ offers not only high standards of entry requirements and reporting, but also an adequate depth and spread of the market to encourage participation of both institutional and retail investors.

In 1997 NASDAQ raised more than seven times the capital raised on the combined equivalent European markets. Carol Galley, Chief Executive of Mercury Asset Management, argues:

> '... we need to improve the efficiency of the capital market for technology based firms. To understand why, one needs to compare the capital markets of Europe with the USA. In recent years, less than a quarter of the investments made by the European venture capital industry were in technology based sectors. By contrast, the USA has managed to channel almost two-thirds of its venture capital funds into technology based firms and currently reaps the benefits of a flourishing technology sector'.[9]

In the European Union a larger share of venture capital is invested in management buy outs (MBOs) or corporate restructuring. MBOs galvanise companies and, when they shed management, can add to the supply of business angels. Until recently, however, investors have adopted a safety first policy towards early stage finance partly because of a perceived high risk in relation to returns obtainable by way of MBOs.

In an important study for the Commission, Graham Bannock has pointed out that attempts to create special sections of national stock markets in Europe have failed to emulate the NASDAQ role model.[10] This has been mainly because they were not sufficiently differentiated from official lists, so investors and issuers regarded them as inferior. Lighter regulations had the consequence of undermining the confidence of investors, leading to a lack of liquidity — and a lack of interest from institutional investors. It must be remembered, however, that NASDAQ has been in existence for over twenty-five years and it was only in the 1980s that IPO listing and share volume growth took off with significant success stories, including Intel and Apple. Many hi-tech stocks could achieve very high price/earnings ratios for several years before showing significant profitability because of the expectation of exponential growth. NASDAQ permitted technology based firms to raise substantial capital sums, allowing some of them, such as Microsoft and Biogen, to become global companies.

New European stock markets

After the stock market crash of 1987, many of the European secondary markets for new issues virtually collapsed. By the early 1990s there were even fewer opportunities for emerging European firms to take advantage of Initial Public Offerings without recourse to NASDAQ. The European markets had to innovate to stay competitive. In 1995, the London Stock Exchange set up an Alternative Investment Market (AIM). In 1997, following an initiative from the European Private Equity and Venture Capital Association (EVCA), prominent venture capitalists and merchant bankers launched the European Association of Securities Dealers Automated Quotation (EASDAQ). The goal of EASDAQ, which is located in Brussels, is to provide a specialist market for hi-tech growth companies — perhaps to become the equivalent of NASDAQ, which, of course, served as its model. EASDAQ, with about forty listings and a market capitalisation of over €16 billion, plans to offer itself for a stock market listing in 2001.

Simultaneously, possibly as a reaction to the conception of EASDAQ, a number of European national markets set up the Euro NM in March 1996 as a framework for new secondary markets. Euro NM has been joined since by SNM (or Nouveau Marché) in France, NMAX (or Nieuwe Markt) in the Netherlands, the Neuer Markt in Germany and Euro NM in Belgium. The association permits the collective communication of stock offerings, but the actual mechanics of trading remain with individual member markets. All the exchanges are member automated, but they utilise different types of systems for undertaking transactions and fixing prices; and the roles of advisers and market-makers can vary from country to country.[11] Euro NM has announced plans to create a common platform bringing in Stockholm, Milan, Zurich and Copenhagen.

Between the London Stock Exchange, NASDAQ and the new European secondary markets, there is healthy competition for new listings. Between EASDAQ and Euro NM, however, there is only marginal competition, and the fragmentation of the market does not engender liquidity. Each of the new markets has strengths and weaknesses. AIM has the most stocks quoted but it tends to be a market for small and medium-sized enterprises (SMEs) with only a quarter in high risk sectors. AIM has been successful in admitting loss-making biotech companies. Euro NM has the largest capitalisation, principally in its French and German associates. If Euro NM can take steps to harmonise its markets further and present a networked platform for trading, it should be able to take advantage of the greater price transparency that will develop as a result of the introduction of the euro. At present, there remain differences in company reporting requirements on the various Euro NM markets. As a recent INSEAD report points out:

> 'Today, there is more potential for abuse of the markets by corporate managers than would be present if reporting requirements were clearer and more harmonised. Slow convergence will not aid the new market in Europe but will act to frustrate the new equity culture.'[12]

EASDAQ, with its pan-European focus, has been a force for the development of cross-border IPOs, which are still not commonplace. It demands international accounting standards, and at all times companies will have a minimum of two market-makers and consequently greater coverage by analysts' reports than other European secondary markets. A strength of NASDAQ — on which EASDAQ companies can also be listed for an additional $20,000 — is its vested interest in providing well researched coverage of the listed stocks. This has been an important factor in the development of institutional investment in venture capital. All this has to be seen in perspective, however. Taken together, the new European markets are a tiny fraction of the size of NASDAQ, and competition remains too limited.

Pressures on the major stock exchanges of the European Union to form alliances make it necessary for a substantial improvement to be achieved in common listing and reporting procedures. It remains to be seen how quickly this will take place and whether the integration will apply to secondary markets. In the meantime, it is to be hoped that both EASDAQ and Euro NM continue to develop strongly.

There is also a need for the consistent policing and regulatory enforcement of both secondary and primary markets. The growth of these new and still somewhat fragile markets could be badly affected by well publicised examples of obvious bad behaviour.[13] A previous Federal Trust report, published in 1993, called for the creation of a new European regulatory agency to be responsible for the regulation of cross-border transactions carried out on wholesale markets by professionals.[14] (The regulation of retail transaction should be best left to national regulators.) The European regulatory agency should be able to carry out its task with a much lighter touch than the US Securities and Exchange Commission, which needs to apply its wider duties across the board in American markets.

As the Commission has recognised 'regulatory fragmentation has a particularly severe impact on risk capital markets'. Extending the jurisdiction of a common EU regulatory agency to the risk capital markets would serve to encourage institutional investment.

Institutional investment

During the past few years there has been an increasing awareness both by a number of member states and by the EU institutions of the need for pump-priming action to increase the supply of venture capital focused in particular on technology based firms.

A Dutch scheme, introduced in 1981, for compensating venture capital companies for 50% of losses on investments achieved its objective of a massive rise in the supply of venture capital, and was discontinued in 1995. Denmark, drawing on the Dutch experience introduced a similar scheme in 1994. In Germany, the two state-owned Federal banks, Kreditanstalt für Wiederaufbau and Deutsche Ausgleichsbank have each launched programmes to make available finance for investment in venture capital and to reduce the risks taken by their private sector partners. In France, programmes to back venture capital funds have been launched by the Caisse des Dépôts et Consignations, using both its own resources and government money derived from the partial privatisation of France Telecom; while the public guarantee agency, Sofaris, is now running a programme to underwrite part of the risk of investors in venture capital funds.

The European Investment Bank (EIB) has played a key role for many years in the modernisation of Europe's physical infrastructure, and, more recently, in urban renewal, health and education projects. In addition, the EIB is itself directly involved in funding venture capital intermediaries under its Amsterdam Special Action Programme, with a particular focus on funds involving the banking sector. The Vienna European Council in December 1998 invited the EIB to accelerate the 'release of funds for risk capital operations' (within the ceiling of €1 billion expected initially to be reached in 2000). For example, the EIB has signed a £20 million loan to Midland Bank which will be invested to promote equity and quasi-equity to a number of small regionally based enterprises in England and Wales.

The European Investment Fund (EIF) was established in 1994 as a partnership between the European Commission, the EIB and financial institutions throughout the Union. In early 1997, the EIF stepped into the field as a 'public institutional investor' providing equity to independently managed funds targeting technology based firms. By early 1999 it had invested some €125 million in twenty-five venture capital funds in ten member states and has the potential to invest €400-500 million in total in this sector. This money is derived from its own capital funds, from funds under management for the EIB and from resources entrusted to it by the European Commission under the Growth and Employment programme launched following the Luxembourg 'employment summit'. The EIF takes minority equity stakes, on average 10-15%, in venture capital funds with well defined investment and exit strategies.[15]

The approach of the EU bodies is to seek to invest only in funds with fully professional management and commercial objectives so as to increase the supply of 'sound money' to the sector. These initiatives are intended to make it easier for venture capital funds to raise the necessary capital and to help draw in private sector investors, in particular institutional investors. Over time such pump-priming should become less necessary.

One factor that will make it so is the higher level of institutional investment activity that would be certain to be engendered by a genuinely integrated pan-European risk capital market. Investors would be attracted as a result of improved accounting standards and better investor protection, as well as ease of trading. The importance of generating such an increase in institutional activity cannot be overstated. As Bannock has observed:

> 'The extent to which pension funds and other institutions increase their holdings in equities in Europe may well be the biggest factor in improving the framework for innovation finance in the future.'[16]

At the moment, Europe remains at a considerable disadvantage vis-à-vis equities in relation to the US in terms of how people save and invest. Europe saves almost half of its total investments in life assurance (17%) and deposits (32%), whereas in the US only one fifth is held in these sectors. The Americans are investing the remaining four-fifths of their savings in a mixture of mutual funds (11%), securities (37%) and pensions (32%). A considerable proportion is then invested in equities which have doubled as a proportion of total financial assets in the years 1990-97. France, Germany and Italy have only 24% of personal sector assets, including pension funds, held in equities, compared with 34% in the USA and 55% in the UK.

The pension time bomb

A major factor behind this disparity is the state of development of the private pensions industry in the US and UK compared to most countries in continental Europe. In 1995 the Federal Trust drew attention to the problem of unfunded deficits in public pension schemes.[17] Brian Corby, who chaired that study group, observed:

> 'Pay-As-You-Go arrangements which provide the bulk of pension provisions in the European Union are underpinned by strong support for the concept of inter-generation solidarity — workers support pensioners in succeeding generations — but it could be dangerous and perhaps wrong to assume that such support will continue in the face of demographic and other changes that can be foreseen.
>
> 'There is an alternative. The firm conclusion of our study is that an increasing share of the cost of retirement should be taken up by privately funded arrangements.'

The projection of existing demographic trends suggests that the ratio of people of working age to the retired population will fall to less than three to one in France, Italy and Germany, countries which already have low pension assets per capita by comparison with the US and the UK. The squeeze on public finance has been institutionalised as a result of EMU and the Stability Pact; the effect of Europe's ageing population compounds the problem, and is leading all EU countries to examine how to shift away from unfunded state pension schemes towards greater private provision.

A report commissioned by the European Federation for Retirement Provision by Koen De Ryck and published in 1996 has calculated that the assets of pension funds could reach over €10,500 billion in 2020, which would be over 70% of the EU's GDP in that year, based on a target coverage of 60% for funded schemes.[18] It is to be noted that this target takes into account the current and expected levels of social security pensions, and the fact that a large number of people are and may continue to be sufficiently covered under these plans because of their salary levels. If Europe's pension fund managers were to set aside for venture capital the same proportion (2%) of their total assets as American fund managers, the funds available by the year 2020 would amount to €210 billion.

Such a level of investment in hi-tech innovation would have a beneficial impact on job creation. Alfred Steinherr, the Chief Economist at the European Investment Bank, has calculated that the ratio between management and capital within the EU is 5000-8000 per €1 billion of capital.[19] The empirical evidence suggests that companies financed by venture capital grow much faster than established businesses. An optimistic calculation, using the upper end of the ratio, would suggest that the EU could generate around 1,700,000 new jobs by the year 2020 as a result of €210 billion being invested by pension funds. Both Silicon Valley and Boston have claimed similar levels of job creation from their successful innovation clusters — which have also taken around twenty years to reach present levels.

In the meantime, pension fund and insurance company legislation has not been harmonised at EU level and restrictions abound regarding the placement of funds by category of asset. The consequence is that institutional investors are generally unable to incorporate the optimal quantities of risk capital and equities in their portfolios. Pension fund managers have also been frustrated from providing schemes which can operate on a pan-European basis by different member state regulations about matching assets and liabilities. One of the effects of the introduction of the euro should be to make currency matching — the minimum proportion of funds that must be invested in the currency in which the pensions should be paid — irrelevant for funds invested in the euro zone.

In America, the growth of NASDAQ was stimulated in the 1970s by exemption from state 'blue sky' laws inhibiting cross state border marketing of securities. The US introduced the Employee Retirement Income Security Act (ERISA) 'prudent man' rule in 1978, which promoted equity investment by institutions. Prudent man regulation placed an obligation on pension fund managers to invest as prudent investors would do on their own behalf, in particular by carrying out sensible portfolio diversification. Australia, Canada, Ireland, the Netherlands and the UK have similar legislation, though the US version seems to give more positive encouragement to funds to diversify into venture investments on a significant scale. The previous Federal Trust report indicated how the EU's draft pension directive could be reworded to achieve a workable agreement across the Union.[20] The European Commission's communication on *Risk Capital* states that:

> 'What is required is sensible, prudential rules that allow pension funds to optimise their portfolio structures with appropriate allocations of pan-European equity, international equity, real estate

and fixed income assets. ... It is very important the Member States ensure that investment restrictions that are allowed under the Treaty for prudential reasons are not used for discriminating against foreign assets nor as an excuse to favour privileged access for the financing of national, regional or local government'.[21]

Business angels

Such reforms of EU regulations and practice for institutional investors would lead to a dramatic improvement in the supply of risk capital in the European Union. Another crucial ingredient of finance for start-up companies receives only a passing reference in the Action Plan, namely, to 'develop networks of business angels at regional, national and community levels'.[22]

Business angels are high net worth, usually self-made individuals with entrepreneurial experience who choose to invest their own money, either individually or as part of an informal syndicate. Colin Mason argues that business angels 'occupy a crucial part of the spectrum of sources of finance for business start-up and expansion, by investing in the 'gap' below which it is uneconomic for venture capital funds to fill because of their cost base and the high transaction costs involved. Their investments are generally small (typically under €150,000) and they mainly invest in businesses at their start-up and early growth stages.'[23] Typically, business angels will be 'hands on' investors, as Mason says, 'using their business experience, skills and contacts to make valuable strategic, monitoring and supportive contributions to their investors' businesses'.

The Commission drew attention to the much greater size of early stage financing in the USA, where there are an estimated 250,000 active individuals investing in between twenty to forty times more businesses than formal venture capital — and five times the amount. Mason estimates that the UK, which has probably the most developed business angel sector in Europe, has approximately 18,000 active and potential angels with current annual investment of around £500 million in about 3500 businesses. Other European countries with a developed business angel sector include Finland, where it is estimated that investments are around 70% of the capital managed by the venture capital industry.

We recognise that there is a strong case for establishing regional networks of business angels (BANs). The British Venture Capital Association's annual review of business angel investment activity confirms the growing volume of investments made through BANs.[24] Mason points out that experience to date indicates that it is not possible for angels to recover the full costs of the BANs' registration fees, and supports the case for some government or corporate sponsorship of BANs. He suggests that the cost to the public purse per job created through BANs has been in the range of €750-1500, a figure that compares favourably with, for example, that of the EU's structural funds.[25]

The Bank of England has also studied the role of business angels in the hi-tech cluster areas of Silicon Valley in California and Boston, Massachusetts.[26] It has discovered that the networks of business angels have close links with venture capital firms, and second and later stage finance is often agreed at the outset. The Bank of England enquiry concluded that such synergy between formal and informal investors should be encouraged in the UK. We would argue the same case even more strongly for the rest of the European Union where business angels tend to be less numerous than in Britain. We also emphasise the importance of the business angel as technology catalyst, providing not only money but also the business and management skills that can transform a start-up company into a really attractive opportunity for the venture capitalist.

A recent Euro-CASE study on engineering and venture capital in Europe has emphasised that business angels are a very valuable source of venture capital and recommends greater harmonisation of fiscal and other incentives in order to boost their role.[27]

We recommend that the role of the European Union should be to galvanise the development of business angels, and that the Commission should become more actively engaged in the inter-regional coordination of BANs. There may be opportunities for modest EU funding of useful, horizontal coordination of technology catalysts.

Patents

The last institutional and market barrier concerns patents. The European Commission calls the overall European patent system as 'profoundly unsatisfactory'. Alongside national patents, there is a European patent which, once granted by the European Patent Office in Munich, operates to all intents and purposes like a national patent. The European Patent Convention of 1978 has nineteen adherent countries, including all EU member states. A single patent application is filed in English, French or German, and is searched, examined, prosecuted and eventually granted as a single patent. (Before 1978, a patent application had to be filed in every country in the language of that country.) To acquire a European Patent is relatively inexpensive, but the problem remains that the Patent must then be registered separately in every country to be effective, and a translation of the specification and claims must be filed in the official language with each national patent office. The latter process is painfully slow and costly. The Commission suggests that the total cost of filing and maintaining a patent in the EU is about ten times that of filing and maintaining a patent in the USA.[28] A European multi-national company, with more than a thousand patent applications a year, faces costs running into millions of euros.

The European Round Table has called for one patent covering the whole EU with the following characteristics:

- a single language system (English, with the possibility to file an application in another official language, but with translation into English);

- a unitary judicial system for enforcement by European courts;

- retention of the existing European and national patent systems to accommodate enterprises having limited geographical interests.[29]

We support the European Commission's new proposal for a regulation on creating a unitary patent valid throughout the EU, for the necessary minimal harmonisation of national rules and procedures, and for other measures to encourage European patent agents to stimulate invention and innovation.

3. Incentives and Taxation

The tax system can have a significant impact on entrepreneurship. It can encourage or obstruct the raising of risk capital, both by entrepreneurs and investors. Given the perceived risks and rewards of investing in early stage high technology companies, tax plays a vital role. High taxation is not conducive to entrepreneurial effort.

The European Commission has emphasised the need for the tax treatment of venture capital funds to be 'as favourable as possible, coherent with other elements of tax regimes applicable to venture capital, and be such as to act as an incentive for their overall development in the EU'.[30] We concur.

The question of taxation is crucial to emerging growth companies at each stage of their development. At the seeding stage, the working proprietors need finance for research and development. Europe's innovating entrepreneurs generally obtain no tax relief on earnings invested in R&D or at the start-up stage when finance is required for product and market development, and when there will typically be no commercial sales, let alone profits and tax payments against which to off-set development costs.

Capital gains tax on the disposal of assets will also be a crucial factor for entrepreneurs. It will also affect remuneration packages, particularly the share options to tempt high quality managers to join high risk, hi-tech ventures. Stock options or employee ownership schemes certainly play a very important role in the USA in motivating executives in technology based firms. They can also help to lower staff costs in a cash-constrained period of development.

We have identified two key problems. First, EU countries tend to tax risk capital at higher levels than the USA. Second, venture capital funds operating across frontiers in the EU can find themselves suffering a double charge of taxation, especially for capital gains. A key objective when structuring a venture capital fund is to avoid double taxation. It is interesting that the UK, which has one of the most favourable legal and fiscal environments in Europe, has also one of the largest venture capitalist industries. The EVCA is calling for a pan-European transparent fund structure that would have similar characteristics to those of a British limited partnership.[31]

American experience

A working group sponsored by the UK Treasury has recognised that the USA provides a useful laboratory on the importance of taxation, particularly capital gains tax, to innovative finance. In 1969 the US rates of capital gains tax (CGT) were increased sharply and the tax treatment of employee stock options was changed so that tax liabilities were incurred when options were exercised rather than when the stock was sold. Start-up finance plummeted. In 1969, the record year, newly formed venture capital partnerships had raised $171 million. By contrast, in 1974-75 members of the US Venture Capital Association managed to raise only $74 million.

In 1979, this policy was reversed, and the maximum CGT rate was cut from 49% to 28%. In addition, after 1981 stock options were taxable when the relevant shares were sold rather than exercised. The market responded with commitments to private equity partnerships in the two years 1980-82 totalling more than $3.5 billion, which was two and a half times more than the entire decade of the 1970s. Over the next three years the same commitment reached more than $4 billion annually, which was yet more than the upturn in the economic cycle implied. The US has continued to develop its CGT regime to encourage entrepreneurial investment. In 1994 the rate was cut from 28% to 14% for holdings lasting five years or longer in small firms. There are also flexible roll-over arrangements which reduce the effective rate on short holds in small companies to zero.

As the European Commission and others have noticed, the supply of venture capital in the US responded dramatically to these changes in tax regime.[32] Also important have been regulatory changes, such as the courts' 1979 decision to extend the prudent man ruling under ERISA to allow venture capital funds to be included in alternative investments.

Graham Bannock has argued that the capital gains tax reductions in the US also acted through the demand side, by encouraging far more engineers and others to act as entrepreneurs. This in turn attracted more funding.[33]

European tax provisions

As Table Three shows, compared to the United States there is a considerable spread of tax rates in EU member states. CGT is relatively high in the UK; in Germany and the Netherlands there is no CGT for private individuals, providing the holding does not exceed a certain percentage. Bannock points out that the euro zone states have a general bias in their tax systems towards tax reliefs for capital investment and, because of high social security contributions, against employment. Prima facie this tendency could be regarded as favouring hi-tech capital intensive companies. In fact, it appears to operate only in favour of the larger firms which have easier access to sources of capital. Working proprietors of small firms generally obtain no tax relief on earnings invested in the equity of their own business. Furthermore, with the exception of Finland and Italy, share options in the European Union are taxed when the options are exercised, whereas in the United States they are charged when the shares are sold. Europe displays a curious bias against the acquisition by individuals of personal wealth through enterprise.

The American experience points to the importance of a low overall rate of capital gains tax from the point of view of encouraging finance into high technology early stage investments. These companies, as has already been noted, carry above average risk and characteristically, in sectors such as biotechnology, require the investor to stay with the share for a lengthy period. The UK government has introduced a tapering in the level of capital gains tax for assets held for long periods, falling from 20% or 40% depending on the tax band to 10% for business assets after ten years. The Treasury's expert group on financing hi-tech businesses, while welcoming these provisions, believes that there is a very strong case for a more radical reform. We recommend special tax incentives for high risk, hi-tech investment.

It is not only the US experience that leads us to that conclusion. The Netherlands, which has a very positive attitude to venture capital, has a CGT regime aimed at encouraging minority shareholdings by both high net worth individuals and corporate investments. There is a

TABLE THREE

Venture Capital in Europe and US

A comparison of some tax provisions

	UK	France	Germany	Italy	Spain	Portugal	Denmark	Belgium	Netherlands	Finland	Sweden	US
Company Tax Rate	30% 20% if profits less than £300000 From 2000, 10% if profits less than £10000	40%	32% on distributed profits, 47% on non-distributed profits	27% to 37% plus local tax of 4.25%	35%	34% to 37.4%	34%	40.17 % with reduced rate for small companies	40% tapering to 35%	28%	28%	35%
Capital Gains Tax Rate for individuals	23% or 40% depending on tax band tapering to 10% for business assets after 10 years With £7100 exemption.	26% subject to F50,000 exemption	Nil for holdings up to 25% - 25.9% to 53% plus 5.5% surcharge	12.5% to 27%	20% to 48%	10% except shares exempt if held for more than 12 months	Up to 58% with some exemption	16.9% with some exemption (Q2 '99)	Nil - 25% if holding over 5% No CGT for holding below 5%	28%	30%	Up to 20% with taper for long-term investors from 2001
Share Options	From 2000 proposed that tax charge when shares sold in certain circ's	Charge mainly when option exercised	Charge mainly when option exercised	Stock plans to employees exempt under certain conditions	Charge when option exercised		Charge generally when option exercised	Charge when option granted (applicable Q2 '99)	Charge when option granted or becomes effective	Charge when option exercised or sold	Charge when option exercised	Charge when shares sold
Tax Incentives for individual investors	EIS and VCTs	Some tax relief for investing in venture capital	No specific provisions	No specific provisions	No provisions		No specific provisions	No provisions	Higher amount of interest tax free if investment in start-up company	No specific provisions	No provisions	No specific provisions

Stated as at 1.2.99. This is only a brief summary and may not cover all situations.

Source: (excl. UK & USA figures) Taxation of Corporate Profits, Dividends and Capital Gains in Europe, Edited by SJ Berwin & Co., EVCA, February 1999

strong case for all EU member states to agree collectively to introduce a CGT regime for hi-tech early stage companies at approximately 20% on gains realised within one year, falling to zero within five years. This schedule would meet the evidence that suggests that business angels exit from their successful investments within an average of five years. A recent paper by Basham and Pickering has pointed out that such CGT reform could also boost the smaller quoted sector.[34]

As we have already noted, the USA changed the way it taxed stock options as long ago as 1981. The UK government proposed in its 1999 budget that in the future small, higher risk trading companies with gross assets of £15 million or less should be able to give key employees a significant amount of tax advantaged equity remuneration, whether in shares or share options, and that a tax charge would normally arise only when shares were sold, and that that charge would be to CGT.

In most of the European Union it remains the case that income tax is charged on the exercise by executives of their share options, irrespective of whether the shares are disposed of at that time. As the EVCA and others have pointed out, the unreformed European tax regime still means that executives can become liable to pay income tax at a time when they do not receive any disposal proceeds (indeed, when they have to pay out money to exercise their options).[35]

Entrepreneurs who establish new companies usually hold shares from their formation and aim to make a capital profit when the company is eventually sold. But it is equally important to attract managerial talent to join early stage companies, and share options at that later stage can be too expensive. Good managers may be reluctant to leave secure employment in larger companies unless they are granted options to acquire shares. The British government appear to have made a sensible contribution towards helping the recruitment and retention of senior executives to small hi-tech firms with its 1999 budget announcement of a forthcoming Enterprise Management Incentive scheme. We recommend a common reform of the European tax regime in this vein so that stock options should be taxed, first, as a capital gain rather than as income and, second, only when they are sold rather than exercised.

Venture capital trusts

The UK's current scheme of personal tax incentives for investment in Venture Capital Trusts has raised over £500 million in the first three years. But only 20% of these funds in 1997-98 went to hi-tech firms and only 19% to early stage companies. The experts reporting to HM Treasury suggested that there would seem to be a powerful case for much greater targeting on the high technology early stage sector which could attract full relief from income tax to investors in the year of their investments as well as CGT exemption after five years.[36] There was also a case for extending VCT reliefs to all institutions, particularly insurance companies, as pension funds already have a tax free base. UK insurance companies currently have around £750 billion under management and if only a small proportion of the total were made available for high technology funds, a significant difference would be made.

The French government has recently announced proposals for encouraging life insurance companies to invest in venture capital. In Belgium, the Cooremann-Deckr Law allows tax deductions for personal investment in shares and special tax incentives for new and expanding companies, with the result that 26,000 enterprises have benefited from the capital provisions. Since 1995 the Dutch government has introduced two tax incentive schemes focusing on small and start-up companies. The first is the 'Aunt Agatha' rule, which provides for a higher amount of interest free of income tax for investing in a start-up company for an eight year period. The Ministry of Economic Affairs is also prepared to contribute one quarter of the total funding of 'techno starter funds'.

European venture capital funds

Although some countries have suitable structures for investment in venture capital, there is no suitable tax structure for these funds to work on a pan-European basis. Several EU countries have funds which are suitable for investing in their own country, but they are limited in what they can invest and are often not suitable for international investors. Other countries have no suitable domestic structure even for investment in their own country. In that case, both the fund's investors as well as its management operation are liable to capital gains and withholding taxes. At present in order to avoid such double taxation, investors from countries without an efficient structure often turn to tax havens, which is far from an ideal solution as the process is costly and fairly cumbersome.

We do not believe that the answer to the present disarray lies in the attempted harmonisation of existing tax situations for venture capital. As we have argued above, if there is a case for tax approximation in the EU it lies in lowering the levels of capital gains tax even to zero rates, and for the taxation of share options to take place at point of sale of the shares in all EU countries. As the EVCA have pointed out, the measure of an efficient venture capital fund structure is that the fund investors should be no worse off than if they had made an investment directly, without the fund as an intermediary. In other words, the tax liability should pass directly to fund investors without the fund first paying taxes on either capital gains or income. Investors should also get any tax credits tied to dividends, and interest and withholding tax should be minimised through the application of double tax treaties.[37]

The European Union must try to create an optional, simplified corporate taxation structure that encourages the development of European hi-tech venture capital funds operating without impediment in more than one member state. National diversity should continue to flourish over questions of tax incentives for retail investors. The main objective for the new technology sector should be to spawn a European market that meets its specific venture capital needs and raises the level of cross-border investments. As the Silicon Valley experience suggests, this state of affairs is likely to be achieved by avoidance of over-regulation.

The Commission's Action Plan on Risk Capital relegates the problem of taxation to a solution in the medium term, and allocates the responsibility for action to member states. We agree with the Commission that the harmonisation of levels of risk capital taxation would be undesirable. As far as taxation structure is concerned, however, we favour a concerted effort to achieve greater transparency in order to avoid the need for any double taxation, and we regard this as an urgent matter. There are strong economic arguments for more coherent and consistent tax structures and bases across the European

Union in order to improve the transparency of tax systems and reduce the costs of entrepreneurship.[38]

We also recommend that the Commission moves to draft a common definition of companies that would benefit from tax incentive schemes.[39] The British Treasury experts have suggested that the qualification might be company and not sector based, as firms with activities that cross the Standard Industrial Classification codes used by the OECD are increasingly common. The Treasury experts suggest that the basis should be the EU definition of a small and medium sized enterprise that spends 10% of its annual sales revenue on research and development of products or services requiring significant technological innovation. Such a common definition would provide a basis for statistical comparisons and benchmarking as well as giving an impetus to much needed tax incentives.

4. Waves and Clusters

The new technological revolution that has swept the world in the last quarter of a century has been typified by groups of American entrepreneurs who have realised the future potential of information technology and biotechnology.

Since the industrial revolution began in the eighteenth century, there have been five waves of new technology pioneered by entrepreneurs in the countries with the right economic, social and political framework conducive to the new innovations taking root. The latest, fifth wave is formed by the convergence of the computer, telecommunications and entertainment industries — and explains America's extraordinary economic performance in the 1990s.

Each wave of technology seems to be characterised by a first phase of 'gales of creative destruction' when the older industries of the previous wave are in decline and when the new industries are subject to rapid technological change and fierce price competition. This phase lasts about twenty five years, during which the successful innovator can be rewarded with exceptional growth and temporary monopoly profits. The spectacular growth and existing high profitability of Microsoft provides a good example of the successful innovator in this phase. In the second phase, the monopoly profits of the original innovators are whittled away by the entry of secondary innovations as the new technology matures and spreads across the whole economy leading to above average productivity gains and a period of prolonged prosperity.

In a previous wave of technological change, the second phase can be traced to the period 1950-74. Then the mass-production techniques which had been pioneered in the USA and were typified by the model T-Ford rapidly diffused into other sectors. Mass production required the evolution of the modern corporation and the development of advertising and marketing techniques to persuade the consumer to buy standardised products. Finally, the Roosevelt administration, faced with an unprecedented economic crisis in the early 1930s, established the New Deal which laid the basis for the infrastructure of roads and suburban life that would cater for an increasingly motorised society.

By the 1950s, Europe, which was recovering from the ravages of World War Two and being helped by the Marshall Plan, was ready to take on board the mass production revolution. In the 1920s the European motor industry, where the fundamental engineering innovations had been developed by the internal combustion engine, had failed to put in place mass production similar to the USA partly because it was making cars for a highly differentiated upper to middle class market. By the 1960s, Europe was experiencing above average growth rates for the OECD countries, particularly in 'technology intensive' industries such as motor vehicles, electrical, chemicals and plastics.[40] High levels of European and world trade stimulated by the Common Market and the Gatt meant that price increases in the growth sectors were now stimulating perceptions of an industrial Golden Age in which Europe led the growth tables.

By 1968 the industrialised countries were suffering the first signs of over-production and declining profitability. Governments on both sides of the Atlantic responded by pump-priming employment, thereby triggering a stock market boom which culminated in the oil price rise and the crash of 1974.

Europe lagging in the new wave

In overall terms, there are not now very significant differences between the EU and the US in terms of birth rates of new businesses as a proportion of the stock of existing businesses. This might suggest that Europe does not lack entrepreneurial dynamism.[41] But Europe has so far been an 'also-ran' in the new wave of technological change. The problem is that Europe's technology based firms tend to remain small. Very few European hi-tech companies can rival US companies in the IT and bioscience industries in terms either of turnover or employees.

In the USA, the phenomenon of rapidly expanding companies such as Intel, Compaq and Microsoft has been fostered by the development of geographic concentrations of hi-tech clusters. Silicon

Valley alone now employs over 1.2 million people. Another long established cluster is around Route 128 in Boston. Israel, too, has developed a dynamic and inevitably concentrated cluster of new technology firms. These hi-tech clusters have generated external economies of scale with the presence of suppliers, skilled personnel and various services, including financial intermediaries. Prominent American universities have been at the centre of these developments, particularly Stanford in California and the Massachusetts Institute of Technology in Boston. A feature of these regional clusters is the propinquity of inventor, entrepreneur, consultant, business angel, technology catalyst and venture capitalist. Michael Porter of Harvard Business School argues that hi-tech clusters are good for productivity, innovation and new business formation.[42] The American experience impressed the Commission:

> 'In Europe there exist few geographic concentrations of high tech clusters of SMEs as compared to the US. Neither are the European clusters as deep nor as integrated as in the US. Networking of SMEs also seems less easy in the EU than in the USA. Yet the ability of companies to tap the best available competencies and resources through flexible co-operation patterns are key assets for innovation and competition. The lack of networking between European research and financial circles is particularly damaging. It accounts for a general lack of understanding and awareness of financing options, increases access times to finance and creates information asymmetries which in turn raise costs'.[43]

Europe retains a much more traditional structure than the USA in which finance, research and production are essentially kept separate. The European Union could, and in our view should, be breaking down these barriers by fostering the dynamic clusters and networks that, as the American story suggests, are clearly needed. To some extent, this requires a change of direction for EU regional policy away from propping up declining areas towards establishing new centres of excellence and knowledge-based growth points in the EU economy.

Encouraged by the European Council, the Commission is moving towards the development of an enterprise policy. As we have seen in Chapter Two, the EIB is now providing risk capital to funds investing in small companies. It would be a logical extension of the EIB's present activities if it expanded its role to support the clustering phenomenon that is identified as being so vital for the future development of European hi-tech. EU-backed investment in networking regions with the latest telecommunications, for example, would stimulate private sector concentration in these regions. Europe's new technology effort has been widely dispersed and needs a re-focusing of intellectual and financial resources upon a number of centres of excellence as well as new initiatives from the public sector. Knowledge based firms benefit from close proximity to each other.

The Cambridge Phenomenon

Cambridge provides Britain's and possibly Europe's closest replica of Silicon Valley. Spawned by the far-sighted policies (and canny investments) of the University and its colleges, the 'Cambridge Phenomenon' is well established, despite some shrinkage, failures and take-overs, particularly in the recession of the early 1990s.[44] Local employment in hi-tech firms has reached about 35,000, whose turnover is between £3-4 billion per annum, of which 36% is generated by exports. There has been a substantial increase in networking between hi-tech companies and consultancies offering advanced business services, and the top five international accountants and three leading local law firms. See Table Four.

By common consent, a certain innocence of the early years of the Cambridge Phenomenon has given way to experience. 'Success was skin deep then. Now Cambridge companies are better able to judge whether their best opportunities lie in licensing or partnership rather than manufacturing', says the senior partner of a leading financial services company.[45] Microsoft's decision to locate its European research centre in the city is a vote of confidence.

Cambridge hi-tech firms have recently provided good returns to venture capitalists. Flotations have been an important boost to business confidence and given credence to share options as a means of recruiting top management without company cash flow suffering too much.

Expectations that continued growth will increase employment by another 25% in the next three years is placing considerable burdens on the physical infrastructure of the area, especially housing and

TABLE FOUR: The Structure of the Cambridge Hi-Tech Cluster 1998

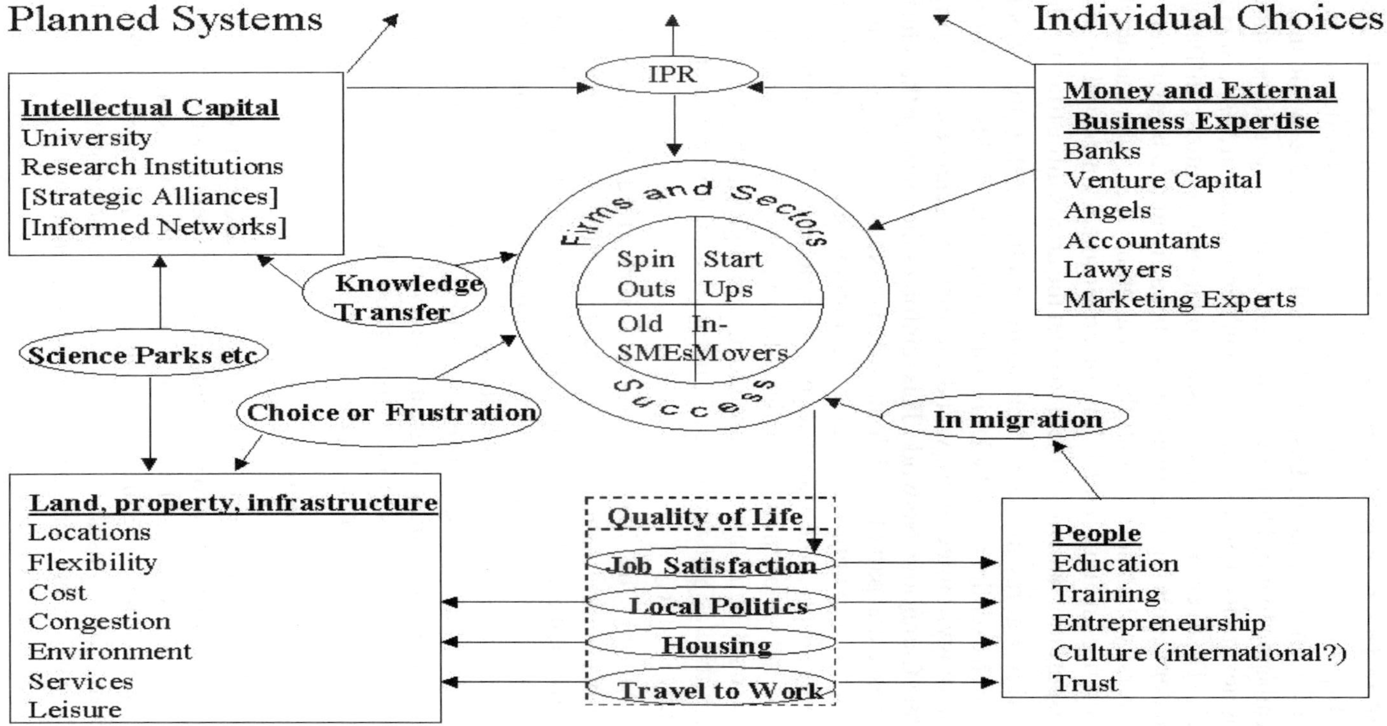

Source: Segal Quince Wicksteed

traffic. The fear is that traditional local government is proving inadequate to the task of keeping up with the challenge. In 1997 South Cambridgeshire District Council refused the Wellcome Trust permission to build a science park that would create another thousand jobs next to its world-leading human genome research site at Hinxton Hall. To overcome these institutional and political difficulties a Greater Cambridge Partnership has been created to bring together the University, business and all the local authorities. The Partnership is becoming an important lobby of government on planning matters, transportation and investment to meet the area's infrastructure deficit.

Key figures in the hi-tech sector itself, which fully reflects the research excellence of the University in the three fields of information technology, biotechnology and the medical sciences, has formed a tighter Cambridge Network. This reinforces the message that clustering is an essential part of hi-tech success. The Network puts great emphasis on the need to improve the area's communications technology, and is helping to promote Cambridge internationally. Hermann Hauser, a prime mover of the Cambridge Phenomenon believes on this basis 'we could build an area around Cambridge of the same order of magnitude as Silicon Valley ... not in five or ten years but maybe in twenty or thirty'.[46]

Among the local conditions identified as necessary for Cambridge's further development are the better provision of entrepreneurial advice to the academic community, special assistance to very small firms, and the training of good managers. The establishment of the University business school should help in this regard. Cambridge also needs a more highly educated workforce in the vicinity, requiring a greater level of investment in local state education. Good schools, like good hospitals, help to attract entrepreneurs and their families.

The Munich power house

In 1945, Bavaria was a war-ravaged backwater without natural resources. In contrast to the Cambridge experience, where little public money has been involved beyond finance for the research base, the Bavarian state government provided a constant stream of funds for research institutes and business development programmes. Official policy was to encourage a culture of enterprise, much associated with

Ludwig Erhard's 'Prosperity through Competition' (1958). Today Bavaria accounts for about half of information technology sales in Germany and is one of the top three bio-science centres in Europe (with Cambridge and Paris).

Like Cambridge, Munich has world famous research centres, such as the Max Planck Institute and the Technical University. Great importance is placed on the promotion of applied research, which is supervised throughout Germany by the Fraunhofer Society, itself headquartered in Munich, supervising a network of seven institutes in Bavaria alone.[47]

State funds are available for the development of science parks and Munich has new business centres located to the north and east of the city. Through its privatisation programme, the Bavarian government has raised DM 5.5 billion that will be invested in 'Offensive Zukunft Bayern' to assist in the development of new businesses, in particular information technology and life sciences. Programmes include loan guarantees for companies lacking security for bank borrowings and funds to provide capital and operating supplies serving the promotion and introduction of innovations. The basis of this support is a public private partnership of holding companies founded by the state government and backed by various private banks and insurers. The provision of equity finance, by for example Bayern Kapital, is dependent on vetting and participation of a private venture capital company. These programmes have encouraged the development of at least five significant venture capital firms based on Munich managing over €1.1 billion. Corporate venturing is also important with Siemens located in Munich providing loans, equity and sales partnerships to local IT companies.

The Bavarian government is very conscious that the region has a long way to go before it can catch up with California. Recently a research and technology development partnership has been set up by the states of California and Bavaria to 'define and implement specific programmes aimed to stimulate partnerships and cross-border investments between the two regions'. The common statement emphasises the importance of IT and biotech clusters in the development process.[48] It also points out that successful software companies internationalise within 2.4 years on average after their founding. It adds:

> 'The importance of speed and strong partnerships in global competitiveness suggests that programmes that accelerate this process contribute significantly to fundamental business growth'.

Role of government

The Munich story suggests that there can be a role for regional government in the provision of the necessary framework conditions for the development of high tech innovations. Fortunately, the lack of regional government in England may about to be overcome with the creation of new regional development agencies (RDAs) in 1999. These bodies are business led, but have a consultative chamber of local government attached. They will focus on strategic coordination, long-term planning, the development of the skills base, and the promotion of inward investment. In time it is anticipated that they will grow into democratically accountable executive authorities with power to coordinate regional policy in trade, housing, transport, health, cultural and environmental matters. We believe that the RDAs will lead to significant economic and political developments in England, as will the new parliaments in Scotland and Wales. Certainly the East of England Development Agency should be welcomed in Cambridge.

The presence of credible, efficient regional government would benefit the development of hi-tech clustering in Europe. In France, the regional council has taken a lively interest in Sophia Antipolis at Nice. The European venture capital market is bound to be attracted not only by good industrial investment opportunities but also to those regions where government is clean, effective and efficient. The more autonomous the regional government from central government constraints, the more its own intrinsic qualities count.

Public funding is better channelled through regional government. The management of the EU's structural and other funds by the Commission and member state governments, especially in the field of education and training, has sometimes lacked precision and control. Regional government is in a better position to provide the analysis and monitoring required by the typical public-private partnership. One option for the EIB would be to assist regional government to develop regional credit facilities for the specific support of hi-tech industry. We would welcome a study of such a proposal, and of how small enterprises might benefit more fully from the lower interest rates of the single currency. The history of the niche market Silicon Valley Bank will be instructive: launched in 1983 it had over 4000 clients and reached market capitalisation of over $500 million by 1997.

Again, lessons can be learned from the US, where a majority of Small Business Investment Companies, set up with public funding to provide early stage financing, failed in the 1980s.[49] The programme was relaunched in 1994 with more flexible leverage available for the larger SBICs and more experienced venture capital management.

In 1998 the then British Secretary of State for Trade and Industry, Peter Mandelson, published a White Paper *Our Competitive Future*, in which the clustering of hi-tech firms featured strongly.[50] The role of government was to 'invest in capabilities', 'catalyse collaboration' and 'promote competition'. It proposes to set up eight university enterprise centres, providing marketing and business skills. Candidates will have to demonstrate how they would become self-financing through fees, royalties or public-private partnerships. Cambridge University has already announced a new school of entrepreneurship along the lines of Stamford and MIT. The entrepreneurship centre at MIT is reckoned to have reversed the trend where most technical spin-outs from the university failed. It is claimed that MIT has now given birth to more than 4000 companies employing 1.1 million people with a turnover of $232 billion a year.[51] We would welcome the widespread development of this approach at universities throughout the European Union.

The encouragement of a new entrepreneurial culture must begin, however, in Europe's schools. For too long European culture has favoured security, stability and equality over risk taking. The European Round Table has drawn attention to the success in Scotland of the Schools Enterprise Programme, which provides educational programmes for schools, colleges and universities 'from primary to plc'. Four-fifths of Scottish schools are participating and two-thirds of 14-18 year olds have been offered enterprise experience. Seven Scottish universities are offering modules in entrepreneurship in every faculty.[52]

5. The Future of Venture Capital in Europe

Venture Capital in Europe is showing signs of entering a 'take off' stage comparable to the American experience in the 1980s. In Germany, where risk capital has been relatively undeveloped, both securities markets and venture capital are developing rapidly. In Britain, which has the most mature venture capital industry in Europe, but where management buy outs have been predominant, the last year has seen over £600 million raised in new funds that are oriented to early stage high technology investment. In France, 1998 witnessed a major change in the private equity environment when restrictions on life assurance fund managers were relaxed allowing them to invest in private equity vehicles and directly in non-listed companies. Finally, we have seen how the European Union is now engaged at the highest level in trying to encourage the development of an integrated venture capital market for the new wave of technologies.

Over-confidence would be a mistake, as it was during the surge in venture capital activity in the late 1980s in Europe when both management and the stockmarkets were disappointed. This time round, however, we detect more realism, as in Cambridge, where the innocence of the 1980s has been replaced by greater experience and harder-headed professionalism. Official attitudes have also changed, and lessons have been learned from the experience of the Delors White Paper of 1993, which failed to be followed through largely because the member states were not prepared to provide the finance.

The Risk Capital Action Plan, unlike the Delors White Paper, does not depend on substantial funding by the member states for its implementation. It does, however, depend on action by the member states to reform substantially the taxation and regulatory framework in order to permit the leap forward in venture capital in Europe of a similar order of magnitude as experienced by the United States in the last two decades.

There is a strong case for all EU member states to cooperate on the reform of their capital gains tax regimes in order to provide low tax rates for hi-tech firms of, say, 20% on gains realised within a year and falling to zero within five years. Stock options should be taxed when sold rather than when exercised. When the US introduced these reforms in the 1980s, venture capital partnerships blossomed. At the same time, there should be rapid progress towards the acceptance throughout the EU of transparent tax structures for investment in venture capital. This would do much to eliminate the need for tax havens.

The European Commission should make a proposal for a common definition of high technology early stage companies that would qualify for the lower rates of CGT and stock options. A common definition of a European venture capital asset class would provide a basis for statistical comparisons and benchmarking, as well as facilitating these much needed tax incentives.

Business angels have played a key role in the development of Boston and Silicon Valley. They provide not only the modest but high risk capital needs of hi-tech firms in their early stages, but also much needed mentoring and shared experience. Their role as catalysts of technology transfer should not be underestimated. In America, the number is still growing of wealthy individuals who have already made substantial fortunes in the new technology clusters and who are prepared to exploit their knowledge and contacts by investing in start-up companies.

There is a clear message here for the European Union. Successful business people should be encouraged by fiscal incentives to become serial investors in start-up companies. The Commission should play an active part in developing regional and inter-regional networks of business angels. Angels should be rewarded where possible by share options in the companies that they can bring to the venture capital market. The synergy between formal and informal investors reminds us how important networking is in the new technologies.

Europe badly needs a liquid risk capital market similar to NASDAQ that has sufficient critical mass to provide exits for venture capitalists and to attract the institutional investor. Otherwise the centre of hi-tech gravity will continue to be across the Atlantic. The Commission's Action Plan is not clear about what needs to be done to gain the evolving European markets the necessary critical mass.

The attempt to set up a Europe wide risk market, EASDAQ, catering specifically for European hi-tech companies has been relatively successful. It has also stimulated the formation of a series of national risk markets under the Euro NM umbrella of which the Neuer Markt in Germany is the most successful. There remains a degree of financial localism which is frustrating the growth of pan-European quotations.

Drawing again from NASDAQ's success, European venture capital needs high standards of critical information and analysis, as well as even handed regulation. It is time to consider the setting up of a European Securities Authority that can insist on necessary common standards and the regulation of the wholesale and risk markets. Such an approach is desirable to encourage institutional investment.

The provision of institutional capital on a much more significant scale is essential to a durable expansion of finance for investment by venture capital funds in innovation-based companies. At the moment, the size of domestic equity in Europe's stock markets in terms of market capitalisation is about one half that of the USA. In the euro zone — without the UK — the size as a percentage of GDP is significantly lower.

The way ahead is to deliver by way of funded pension schemes an increasing share of the cost of retirement. The EU's Competitiveness Advisory Group recently reinforced the point by recommending 'urgent action to incentivise and re-regulate the financial restructuring that is required in several member states before take-off of a robust, sound pension fund sector integrated into a pan-European pension market can occur.'[53] Assuming the large growth of funded schemes, we have seen in Chapter Two how dramatic the effect on employment could be if Europe invested the same proportion of its pension funds in venture capital as the United States. It is difficult to know how European hi-tech can be the world challenger in the absence of such a development.

This report wishes to underline the importance of hi-tech clusters in generating external economies of scale and creating an environment for innovation and growth. We consider that this development must be given the highest priority by the European Union. Cambridge and Munich have already demonstrated what can be achieved by linking up academic centres of excellence, innovatory companies and networks of venture capital finance and other corporate and legal advice.

For the European Union this requires a change of orientation. While it must continue to concern itself with ameliorating disparities of economic opportunity, it must also refocus its mechanisms of financial support towards the further development of centres of innovation.

We propose that the EU should borrow from the British white paper on competitiveness and initiate a science enterprise challenge for Europe with a view to creating around twenty university enterprise centres. The successful centres should be endowed with a Jean Monnet chair of entrepreneurship and donated some seedcorn money with which to stimulate spin-offs by the academic staff. At the same time, the EIB along with the relevant national and regional authorities should be encouraged to finance public-private partnerships with a view to establishing or reinforcing the clustering phenomenon around centres of scientific excellence.

In addition, the European Union, through its market oriented intermediaries, should continue to make money available for pump-priming purposes in technology-oriented venture funds, including those in appropriate regions. The funds should have a substantial involvement of the private sector, both commercial and professional, must have identified clear market opportunities, and must draw on local knowledge and support.[54] The EU could also do more to help in the development of infrastructure for science parks and technology clusters.

These are our recommendations for the future of European venture capital. With these reforms, and others in the sphere of labour and industrial innovation, and with continued investment in education, the European Union will be sure to have nurtured and profited from some of the world's leading new technologies as we surf the fifth wave. We hope that the drive to build such an Entrepreneurial Europe will be the central agenda of the next European Commission.

NOTES

[1] For a lively analysis of the American story, see 'Innovation in Industry', Survey in *The Economist*, 20 February 1999.
[2] One exception to this general rule is Nokia — and a remarkable one: there will be some 500 million mobile phones worldwide in 2000, although the industry is less than twenty years old. See High Technology Finland 1999, Finnish Academies of Technology and the Finnish Foreign Trade Association, Helsinki, 1998.
[3] European Commission White Paper, *Growth, Competitiveness, Employment: the challenges and ways forward into the 21st century*, Supplement to EC Bulletin, 6/93.
[4] OECD Jobs Strategy, *Technology, Productivity and Job Creation*, Paris, OECD, 1998.
[5] European Commission, *Risk Capital: A Key to Job Creation in the European Union*, April 1998, p. 1.
[6] In this respect, we commend the report from the European Round Table, *Job Creation and Competitiveness through Innovation*, Brussels, November 1998.
[7] Adapted from Mark van Osnabrugge, *Comparison of Business Angels and Venture Capitalists: Financiers of Entrepreneurial Firms*, Venture Capital Report and Said Business School, Oxford, July 1998.
[8] *Financing of High Technology Businesses: A Report to the Paymaster General*, HM Treasury, November 1998.
[9] Carol Galley, *The UK R & D Scoreboard*, Department of Trade and Industry, 1998. It is important to note, however, that definitions of venture capital differ between US and European norms.
[10] Bannock Consulting, *Innovation Finance in Europe: A Pilot Project in Benchmarking*, for DG III and DG XIII of the European Commission, 1998. The study involved all EU member states, and compared conditions in the USA, Israel and the EU.
[11] See Daniel F. Muzyka, Benoit Leleux, Nathalie Guegan, *European New Issues Markets: A Preliminary Review*, INSEAD for 3i Venturelab, November 1998.
[12] Ibid.
[13] Ibid.
[14] Dick Taverne, *Towards an Integrated European Capital Market*, Federal Trust Study Group under Chairmanship of Lord Howe of Aberavon QC, March 1993.
[15] Gerbrand Hop, 'Venture Capital for creating new jobs in Europe', speech to the EIB Forum, London 1998.
[16] Bannock, op. cit., p. 18.

[17] Dick Taverne, *The Pension Time Bomb in Europe*, Federal Trust, 1995.
[18] Koen De Ryck, *European Pension Funds*, Report commissioned by the European Federation of Retirement Provision, 1996.
[19] Alfred Steinherr, *The role of investment for creating jobs*, EIB Forum, October 1998.
[20] Taverne, 1995, op.cit.
[21] *Risk Capital*, op. cit, p. 13.
[22] European Commission, *Risk Capital: Action Plan*, June 1998, p. 2.
[23] Colin M. Mason and Richard T. Harrison, 'Public Policy and the Development of the Informal Venture Capital Market: UK experience and lessons for Europe' in K. Cowling (ed.), *Industrial Policy in Europe*, London, Routledge, forthcoming.
[24] British Venture Capital Association, *Report on Business Angel Investment Activity 1996-97*, London, BVCA, 1997.
[25] Rudy Aernoudt, 'European policy towards venture capital: myth or reality' in *Venture Capital*, Vol. 1, No. 1, 1999.
[26] Adrian Piper and Melanie Lund, *Finance for Small Firms: a visit to the United States*, Bank of England Business Finance Division (unpublished), July 1997.
[27] EuroCASE, *Engineering and Venture Capital in Europe*, European Council of Applied Sciences and Engineering, November 1998.
[28] European Commission, *First Action Plan for Innovation in Europe*, Supplement to EC Bulletin, 3/97.
[29] European Round Table, op. cit.
[30] *Risk Capital*, op. cit, p. 17.
[31] EVCA White Paper, *Priorities for Private Equity: Realising Europe's Entrepreneurial Potential*, Brussels, EVCA, April 1998.
[32] P. Gompers and P. Lerner, 'What Drives Venture Capital Fundraising?', Harvard University and National Bureau of Economic Research. Paper presented at Brookings Institution Conference, June 1998.
[33] Bannock, op. cit
[34] Brian Basham and Craig Pickering, *Tomorrow's Giants*, Equity Development, March 1999.
[35] EVCA Special Paper, *Stock Options*, edited by S.J. Berwin & Co, Brussels, EVCA, March 1999.
[36] HM Treasury, op. cit.
[37] EVCA White Paper, op. cit.
[38] For a wider discussion of tax issues, see Federal Trust Report, *The Future of Corporate Tax in the European Community*, London, Federal Trust with Kogan Page, 1991.
[39] The Commission is already undertaking a pilot scheme to develop the technology rating of hi-tech companies.

[40] C. Freeman, J. Clark, L. Soete, *Unemployment and Technical Inovation: A Study of Long Waves and Economic Development,* Science Policy Research Unit, Sussex Unversity, 1982.
[41] Bannock, op. cit.
[42] See Michael E. Porter, 'Clusters and the New Competitive Agenda for Companies, Governments and Institutions' in *On Competition*, Harvard Business School Press, 1998.
[43] *Risk Capital*, op. cit., p. 17.
[44] Segal Quince Wicksteed, *The Cambridge Phenomenon*, 1985; and *The Cambridge Phenomenon Revisited: a study to explore the dynamics of business growth*, (forthcoming).
[45] B. Groom, 'Cambridge Overview: High-tech sector has a broader base this time', Financial Times, 16 July 1998
[46] Ibid.
[47] Bavarian Ministry for Economic Affairs, Transport and Technology, *Research and Technologies in Bavaria*, Munich, 1996.
[48] State of California and Free State of Bavaria, *California-Bavaria*, Research and Technology Development Partnership, 1998.
[49] Pascale Viala, *Financing young and innovative enterprises in Europe: Supporting the venture capital industry*, EIB Papers, Vol. 3, No. 1, 1998.
[50] DTI White Paper, *Our Competitive Future: Building the Knowledge Driven Economy*, Cmnd 4176, London, HMSO, December 1998.
[51] 'Ancient and Modern', *The Economist,* 19 December 1998.
[52] Ibid.
[53] See the Report of the EU Competitiveness Advisory Group to the European Council, *Capital Markets for Competitiveness*, June 1998
[54] One such example already supported by the EIF is that of Scottish Equity Partners, who are linked to the government development agency Scottish Enterprise.

APPENDIX

EU Action Plan, June 1998

I. MEASURES IN PROGRESS

Measures	**Responsibility / participation**
MARKET FRAGMENTATION	
Develop networks of business angels at regional, national and Community levels	Private sector Member States Commission
Market monitoring and development of information and statistics on all levels of venture capital in the EU	Commission EVCA market players
INSTITUTIONAL AND REGULATORY BARRIERS	
Transposal and implementation of all financial services directives - monitoring via single market scoreboard	Member States Commission
Simplification of administrative formalities for company formations (including minimum capital requirements)	Member States Commission (disseminating best practice)
PAUCITY OF HIGH-TECH SMALL BUSINESSES	
Development of networking and clustering between universities, research centres, financial backers, lawyers, human resource specialists etc., and link them at European level	Private sector Member States Commission (pilot schemes, disseminating best practice, Vth Framework Research Programme)
HUMAN RESOURCES	
Promotion of entrepreneurship and innovation within educational and training systems	Member States Commission (disseminating best practice)
CULTURAL BARRIERS	
Demonstration of the advantages of venture capital and promotion of entrepreneurship	Private sector Member States Commission

II. MEASURES TO BE LAUNCHED IN THE SHORT TERM

Measures	Objectives	Responsibility / Participation	Schedule
MARKET FRAGMENTATION			
Round table on the impact of the fragmentation of the European risk capital market	Prompt all the market players to generate synergy to reduce the effects of fragmentation	Commission Member States Market players (regulatory bodies, new capital markets, venture-capital funds, banks, etc.)	October 1998
Detailed examination of the cost to European firms of raising debt and equity finance	Obtain a clearer picture of the difficulties and financial needs of firms	Commission Market players (banks, venture-capital funds, capital markets, etc.)	Study to be launched in 1998
INSTITUTIONAL AND REGULATORY BARRIERS			
Venture-capital funds: assessment of whether there is a need for Community legislation covering specific closed-end funds	Create, along the lines of Directive 85/611 on UCITS, a European passport for closed-end funds (including venture-capital funds), enabling them to raise funds and offer their services in all Member States without restriction	Commission Council EP Industry: EFIFC EVCA small business	Work to start end 1998
Review of implementation and possible amendment of prospectus directive to facilitate companies raising cross-border capital (eg. IPOs)	In these areas, a prospectus or offer document approved in one Member State should be available for use in all the Member States	Commission Council EP Capital markets (competent authorities/small businesses)	Work to start end 1998

PAUCITY OF HI-TECH SMALL BUSINESSES

Creation of a pan-European club of high-tech innovatory firms	Facilitate dissemination at European level of examples of successes and good practice: facilitate contact with investors	Market players (small businesses, venture-capital funds, etc.) Commission	To be launched end 1998
Reform of the European patent system	Following on from the Green Paper, simplify procedures and create a genuine Community patent	Commission Member States EP	Proposal end 1998

HUMAN RESOURCES

Determination of training needs for venture-capital fund managers, market makers, analysts of high-tech firms	Identify training schemes to be set up to make good any shortages of skilled staff in these areas	Commission Market players	Study to be launched end 1998
Assessment of benefits of equity pay and employee ownership schemes	Begin study of future at European level	Member States Commission Social partners	1998-99

CULTURAL BARRIERS

Dissemination of best practices in corporate governance	Facilitate the dissemination of corporate governance practices demanded by investors	Private sector International bodies Commission Member States	1998-99

III. ORIENTATIONS FOR THE MEDIUM TERM

INSTITUTIONAL AND REGULATORY BARRIERS

Measures	Objectives	Responsibility / Participation
Adoption of prudential rules to allow institutional investors to invest in venture capital	Allow institutional investors, acting in accordance with 'prudent man' rules, to invest in venture capital	Member States Commission (follow-up to the Green Paper on supplementary pensions)
Assess existing accounting and auditing requirements	Allow companies to draw up consolidated accounts to facilitate access to risk capital (for IPOs and listed companies)	Member States Commission Accounting Bodies
Reduction of the capital requirements for setting up firms	Facilitate the setting up of firms	Member States
Reform of the legislation on insolvency and bankruptcy	Whilst protecting the interests of creditors and consumers, ensure that entrepreneurs who have gone bankrupt can have a second chance	Member States Commission (dissemination of best practice)

TAXATION

Themes	Issues to consider	Responsibility
Taxation of venture capital funds	Double taxation	Member States
Capital gains tax	Impact on venture capital	Member States
Stock options	Impact on recruitment and company performance	Member States
Tax arrangements for new firms	Fiscal environment for start-ups	Member States
Taxation of low-risk capital (eg. bank deposits, bonds) compared with venture capital	Situation in Member States	Member States